A. N. Towne

An Open Letter to the United States Senate Committee

On Relations with Canada

A. N. Towne

An Open Letter to the United States Senate Committee
On Relations with Canada

ISBN/EAN: 9783337154752

Printed in Europe, USA, Canada, Australia, Japan

Cover: Foto ©ninafisch / pixelio.de

More available books at **www.hansebooks.com**

TO THE

UNITED STATES SENATE COMMITTEE

ON

Relations with Canada.

BY

A. N. TOWNE,

Third Vice-President and General Manager
Southern Pacific Company.

WITH SOME REMARKS ON THE FOURTH AND FIFTH
SECTIONS OF THE INTERSTATE COMMERCE LAW.

SAN FRANCISCO, JUNE 20th, 1889.

SAN FRANCISCO,
H. S. CROCKER & CO., STATIONERS AND PRINTERS,
1889.

AN OPEN LETTER

TO THE

UNITED STATES SENATE COMMITTEE

ON

Relations with Canada.

BY

A. N. TOWNE,

**Third Vice-President and General Manager
Southern Pacific Company.**

WITH SOME REMARKS ON THE FOURTH AND FIFTH SECTIONS OF THE INTERSTATE COMMERCE LAW.

San Francisco, June 20th, 1889.

SAN FRANCISCO,
H. S. CROCKER & CO., STATIONERS AND PRINTERS,
1889.

To the Honorable Members

of the United States Senate Committee

on Relations with Canada,

Gentlemen : On your recent visit of investigation to the Pacific Coast, in the matter submitted to you by the Senate of the United States, you honored me by presenting a series of questions bearing on the subject in hand, with a request for my answers thereto, also permitting me to give expression to my opinions and the result of my experience regarding the unhealthy competition forced on American railroads by our neighbors to the northward. I must confess that in this connection I was astounded to discover how little the public at large had studied this question, and how slightly our people appreciated the danger threatened to American interests by Canadian competition in American transportation. I had supposed that thinking men had at least given the matter a superficial consideration ; but it remained for the awakening of public interest, by the visit of your Committee, to convince me of my error in this regard.

The publication through you of even the more salient facts has aroused the active interest of many thinking men, where before there had been but apathy ; and it developed that those who, either on account of their personal interests or as a matter of political principle, are staunch advocates of a high protective tariff as the basis of our commercial and industrial prosperity, had never stopped to think that unequal competition with foreign railroads, constructed and operated under conditions inimical to us, was as dangerous to the country as competition with foreign wool or with foreign products of cheap

3

labor. It did not occur to them that the invested capital and widely ramified interests involved in the great transportation system of the United States were threatened with disaster relatively as serious as the most positive protectionist could predict in case of a Governmental free-trade policy.

Although much of public importance has been said and written on the subject by railroad scientists, it has mostly reached the ears and eyes of railroad men, but has not been brought into touch with the public pulse ; for the American people, as a rule, are so self-confident in their wonderful prosperity and the power and resources of their country, that they are careless of danger unless actually confronted with it ; and it is not until then they arise in their might against interference or aggression. The Samoan episode, just brought to a happy and honorable conclusion by the force of American determination as much as by our admirable diplomacy, is a notable recent instance of this spirited American characteristic, and of the respect entertained for it by the most powerful countries of Europe when deliberately asserted.

It is because of this arousal of public sentiment as observable in California, and because my mail is crowded with requests for information and data, that I am impelled to address your Honorable Committee in this form that I may thereby be enabled to cover broader ground. I beg to assure you, gentlemen, that I do not undertake this task frivolously or for the sake of work. I assume it rather as a duty to the vast transportation interests of our country; and not less a duty to those hundreds of thousands who, not directly connected with transportation problems, have their savings—the thrifty accumulation of provident years—invested in railway securities ; to those other thousands, the innocent ones whose all is tied up in those securities set aside for them in loving forethought ; to the millions who through their employment in the various fields of labor or their mercantile connections, are affected by whatever either depresses or stimulates railway properties; while I deem it a subject fraught with deep importance to this country and its people, and will endeavor to consider it with freedom from personal bias, self-interest or any motive except the ultimate weal of the great nation of which I am proud to be a citizen.

I will risk the charge of being abruptly intrusive by reproducing at this stage the questions propounded to me by your Committee and my answers thereto, as per copy on file with your Honorable body. I do so, because, in my judgment, they strike the key-note to the danger now menacing us, namely, embarrassment, financial and industrial, through arbitrary legislative railway regulation of a kind unknown and intolerable in any other industry or commercial undertaking, and whose whole tendency is to cripple instead of stimulate beneficent enterprises ; the railways thus restricted being yet called upon to face the competition of foreign carriers, and expected to cope with them effectually under conditions which seem to preclude the possibility of success.

QUESTIONS PROPOUNDED TO A. N. TOWNE BY THE UNITED STATES SENATE COMMITTEE ON RELATIONS WITH CANADA, AND THE ANSWERS THERETO :

Question 1. Please state your name, residence and occupation ?

Answer.—A. N. Towne, Third Vice-President and General Manager of the Southern Pacific Company. My residence is in San Francisco.

2. How long have you been connected with the Southern Pacific Company, and in what capacities ?

A.—I came to California twenty years ago to accept the position of General Superintendent of the Central Pacific Railroad Company, since leased to the Southern Pacific Company. Prior thereto I was connected with roads in Illinois for fourteen years ; one year on the Chicago and Great Eastern, as General Superintendent, and thirteen years on the Chicago, Burlington and Quincy Road, occupying positions, passing through all the grades in the management of transportation to that of Assistant General Superintendent.

3. State what trans-continental lines of railroad are now in operation, terminating at San Francisco, what at Portland, Oregon, and what upon Puget Sound and the Gulf of Georgia. Also, what other, if any, carriers are engaged in trans-continental traffic ?

A.—Trans-continental lines—commencing at the north we have the Canadian Pacific Railway, terminating upon the Gulf of Georgia, at Vancouver, B. C., using in connection with its road the Pacific Coast Steamship line of steamers to and from San Francisco. The next is the Northern Pacific rail line, terminating at Tacoma, W. T., and Portland, Oregon; also using the Pacific Coast Steamship Company's steamers to and from San Francisco, via Tacoma. The Northern Pacific also forms a through line to San Francisco and adjacent cities in California, via the Southern Pacific Company's road from Portland. Then comes the Oregon Railway and Navigation Company, terminating at Portland. This road, in connection with the Oregon Short Line and the Union Pacific Railway, forms a through line to the Missouri River; between Portland, Or., and San Francisco, this line uses its own steamers to form a through line to and from San Francisco. The Canadian Pacific, Northern Pacific and Oregon Railway and Navigation Companies each have a line also to California ports south of San Francisco, by their use of the Pacific Coast Steamship Company's steamers, thus being able to reach, notably, San Diego, San Pedro (the port of Los Angeles), and Santa Barbara. Our Southern Pacific Company's line extends from Portland, Or., to San Francisco, passing Roseville, Cal., where a junction is formed with the Central Pacific Railroad, direct to Ogden, there connecting with the Union Pacific and the Denver & Rio Grande Western Railway, who respectively have various Eastern rail connections. From San Francisco south the Southern Pacific Company forms a through line with the Atlantic and Pacific road at Mojave, which connects with the Atchison, Topeka, and Santa Fe road at Albuquerque, N. M., for the Missouri river and Eastern points. From Mojave south the Southern Pacific Company has, via Los Angeles, another connection with the Atchison, Topeka and Santa Fe road at Deming, N. M., and also connects at El Paso, Tex., with the Texas and Pacific Road, and through it with the Missouri Pacific system. From El Paso the Southern Pacific Company's line runs to New Orleans, there connecting with its own line of steamships for ports on the Atlantic seaboard. We also connect at Houston, Tex., San Antonio, Tex., and New Orleans, La., with several lines of railroad by which we have connection with various Eastern cities. Other carriers and important ones are the Pacific Mail Steamship Company, between San Francisco and Eastern Atlantic seaboard points, via Panama, as well as the clipper lines, via Cape Horn, between Portland and San Francisco and the port of New York, all strong competitors against the overland rail carriers.

4. Please state, if you know, what companies are engaged in the running of steamships between the Pacific Coast and ports in China and Japan?

A—The Pacific Mail Steamship Company's steamers and the Occidental and Oriental Steamship Company's steamers ply between San Francisco and ports in China and

Japan. The Canadian Pacific Steamship Company's steamers ply between Vancover, B. C., and ports in China and Japan.

5. Has there been, at any time, and, if so, when and for how long, any other steamship company engaged in said trade?

A.—During the past fourteen years no steamship company, other than those enumerated in answer to the interrogatory preceding, has, to our knowledge, operated between the Pacific coast and ports in China and Japan.

6. What steamships are owned by the Pacific Mail Steamship Company, in which trade are they engaged, between what ports do they ply, and how frequent are their trips?

A.—The Pacific Mail Steamship Company's steamers are: City of Peking, City of Sydney, City of New York, and City of Rio de Janeiro. The Occidental and Oriental Steamship Company's steamers are: Belgic, Gaelic, Arabic and Oceanic. The steamers of both these lines ply between San Francisco and ports of Yokohama, Japan, and Hongkong, China, with steamer connections for other ports in Japan and China. The Pacific Mail and Occidental and Oriental steamers make alternate trips in both directions: their combined sailings averaging three steamers a month in each direction. Attached, marked "Exhibit A," is the printed list of sailings of these steamship companies outward bound from November 28, 1888, to December 31, 1889, and homeward bound from January 8, 1889, to February 6, 1890, both, of course, subject to such changes as the necessities of the traffic may demand.

7. State, generally, the character of the trade in which they are engaged.

A.—The steamers plying between San Francisco, California, and ports in China and Japan, are engaged in a general passenger and freight traffic. The principal exports are flour and specie. The imports are tea, raw and manufactured silk, rice, gunnies, hemp, jute and general merchandise.

8. Please state, if you know, what company is engaged in running steamships between Vancouver and ports of China and Japan.

A.—The so-called Canadian Pacific Steamship Company runs a line of steamers between Vancouver and ports in China and Japan.

9. What steamships are owned and controlled by that company, between what ports do they ply, how frequent are their trips, and what is the general character of the trade in which they are engaged?

A.—The steamers owned or controlled by the Canadian Pacific Railway are : Abyssinia, Parthia, Port Augusta, Batavia and Port Fairy, plying between Vancouver, B. C., and the ports of Yokohama; Japan, and Hongkong China, with steamer connections for other ports in China and Japan, and competing with steamers of the Pacific Mail and Occidental and Oriental Companies in every Asiatic port at which the latter companies have sought business. Their schedule of sailings is, I believe, as per " Exhibit B," herewith, outward bound from May 14, 1889, to November 29, 1889, and homeward bound from April 4, 1889, to October 24, 1889. They engage in general passenger and freight traffic. The principal exports are flour and cotton goods, otherwise known as domestics, the Canadian Pacific having already been successful in diverting from United States lines almost the entire cotton-piece-goods trade of the Eastern States. The principal imports are tea, raw and manufactured silk, rice, gunnies, hemp, jute and general merchandise. They compete with the American steamer lines named to and from the port of San Francisco in every item of traffic in which the San Francisco lines are engaged, except perhaps, from financial causes, the single item of American specie. The

Canadian Pacific Railway also runs its own steamers on the great lakes. I am not acquainted with the names of the steamers or the frequency of their trips, but understand they are operated in conjunction with the Canadian Pacific rail line to afford the most feasible connections with points on the great lakes.

10. State, if you know, what Government aid, if any, said company has received or is receiving.

A.—I understand the Dominion Government has granted the Canadian Pacific Railway a subsidy or bonus of $25,000,000; has donated to it 25,000,000 acres of land, embracing only such as are suitable for settlement; has also given right of way, station grounds, dock privileges and water frontage, in so far as within the control of the Government; and, further, has constructed and transferred to the Canadian Pacific Railway Company, free of cost, 714 miles of railway, the estimated value of which, according to that railway company's report for the year 1887 is $35,000,000. The Canadian Pacific was permitted to import steel rails free of duty, also other material used in the construction of its road and telegraph line. Under its charter, the Canadian Pacific is freed for all time from taxation by the Dominion Government or by any Provincial Government established after date of its charter. Its land grant in the northwest territory is free from taxation for twenty years unless sold in the mean time. In addition to all this the Canadian Government has bound itself not to permit, during the term of twenty years, the building of any line or lines that would parallel the Canadian Pacific Railway. This we believe to be the most liberal grant ever bestowed by a constitutional Government.

11. State whether or not any freight shipped at San Francisco for Boston, New York, and other Atlantic ports of the United States, is shipped via the Canadian Pacific Railway ; if so, about how much, and by what transportation lines is it transported to the Pacific terminus of said road ?

A.—As per my answer to third interrogatory, the steamers of the Pacific Coast Steamship Company are used by the Canadian Pacific Railway for transporting its freight between San Francisco, Cal., and Vancouver, B. C. After the completion of the Canadian Pacific Railway, that company made arrangements to reach San Francisco by means of the steamers of said steamship company, and have ever since sought and obtained a share of east-bound through traffic. For example: In 1887 their east-bound through freight from San Francisco, via Vancouver, amounted to 7,274 tons, including several million pounds of sugar, also large quantities of wool, leather, hides, beans and dried fruit.

During the sixteen months from January 1, 1888, to April 30, 1889, the Canadian Pacific secured a tonnage of some ten million pounds from the following principal items of east-bound shipment : Wool, sugar, canned goods, borax, canned and pickled salmon, hides, horns, leather, beans, wine, dried fruit and prunes, mustard seed, cocoa, coffee and logs. Thus :

	POUNDS.
Wool	5,029,243
Sugar	1,099,091
Canned goods	1,701,633
Borax	328,070
Salmon, canned and pickled	264,860
Hides	81,515
Horns	153,626
Leather	146,800
Beans	143,750
Wine	91,830
Dried fruit and prunes	375,152
Mustard seed	56,745
Cocoa	25,700
Coffee	50,877
Logs	375,960

This freight was for points in the United States east of the Mississippi river, chiefly Atlantic seaboard cities and cities east of and including Chicago.

The efforts put forth by the Canadian Pacific Railway to secure the west-bound freight are, we have reason to believe, not less active than those employed in securing east-bound tonnage; but it is very difficult for us at this western end—who handle none of the west-bound traffic of that foreign route—to determine with any degree of precision the extent and value of their west-bound business, from eastern to western United States points. We have been able to ascertain, however, that in 1887 that company carried not more than 5,500,000 pounds of such west-bound freight, while in the year 1888 they increased their traffic to an amount not less than 13,750,000 pounds in the aggregate; and our best advices indicate that we need not be surprised if the extraordinary ratio of increase thus indicated should, under existing circumstances, be greatly exceeded for 1889. As illustrative of the probability, I may cite that an examination of the manifests of the Pacific Coast Steamship Company's steamers arriving at this port from Vancouver with freight, ex Canadian Pacific Railway, show that, during the first four months of 1888, there were brought here by that route, 20,059 packages, the weight of which we cannot determine; whereas, during the first four months of 1889, the number of packages so landed here has increased to 88,376 packages.

12. Please state what steam or other vessels are engaged in transporting between San Francisco and British Columbia.

A.—The Oregon Railway and Navigation Company's steamers to Portland, with connecting steamers northward; the Pacific Coast Steamship Company and the Wells' line of clippers and steam coasters are, I believe, the only transportation lines regularly plying between San Francisco and British Columbia, although there are probably other sailing and steam coasting craft engaged in the traffic. For a time the Canadian Pacific steamers to and from China and Japan ran to and from Vancouver via San Francisco, calling here on each trip, and may do so again when they deem it expedient.

13. What efforts are made and what inducements offered by the Canadian Pacific Railway to secure the shipment of freight from San Francisco to Atlantic ports of the United States by its road?

A.—On August 18, 1886, the Canadian Pacific Railway announced the establishment at San Francisco of a general agency, for the securing of freight and passenger traffic, a General Agent being then appointed to actively enter the field for business. That general agency is still maintained, and has at all times since that date been actively competing for the overland traffic.

The inducements offered are careful attention to the traffic and quick time, coupled with a lower rate when shipments are made by the Canadian Pacific Railway, than when made by the American rail lines. At the present time the relative rates charged, for example, to the Atlantic seaboard points—New York, Boston, Philadelphia, etc.—by the American lines and by the Canadian Pacific are as follows, governed by the Western claassification, like class-rates and like differentials applying also on overland freight shipped from the Eastern to the Pacific States:

AMERICAN LINES.

1	2	3	4	5	A	B	C	D	E
420	370	295	230	200	200	180	145	130	120

CANADIAN PACIFIC RAILWAY.

1	2	3	4	5	A	B	C	D	E
380	335	270	210	180	185	165	133	120	112½

To illustrate by commodities: The rate on grease wool, compressed in bales, from San Francisco to New York by the American rail lines, is $1.50 per 100 pounds, while shipments by the Canadian Pacific are charged $1.38 per 100 pounds, being a differential of 12 cents in favor of the Canadian Pacific. By the American rail lines canned goods, in carloads, to New York are charged $1.20 per 100 pounds, while shipments by the Canadian Pacific are charged $1.10 per 100 pounds.

During the sixteen months ending April 30, 1889, the Canadian Pacific carried from San Francisco to St. Paul 1,099,091 pounds of sugar, at a rate of 60 cents per 100 pounds, while the rail lines in the United States would charge 65 cents per 100 pounds thereon.

These differential rates which the United States roads were compelled to accord the Canadian Pacific Railway were devised as the best available plan for preventing that foreign competitor from practically destroying the through traffic of the United States roads, because, the Canadian Pacific's local business not being subject to the interstate commerce law, they are in a position to absolutely dictate and control the rates at which the United States lines may carry through traffic, by simply underbidding United States lines and pursuing that policy until they obtain a recognition which their geographical position and commercial influence could not themselves secure.

It may be true that, theoretically, the Canadian Pacific Railway is subject to the interstate commerce law on interstate traffic passing to or from Canada. But it is obvious that, while the United States roads are subject to all the restraints the Interstate Commerce Act imposes, it is impossible for this Government to hold the Canadian Pacific Railway to an observance of the law; for the United States can have no jurisdiction over the rates charged on intermediate business picked up and laid down in Canada, which, together with the relatively small amount interchanged between points in Canada and the United States, amounts to 96 per cent of that company's entire earnings, according to a published letter from the President of that company.

The Canadian Pacific Railway can thus make rates on through business without interfering with its earnings on traffic between Vancouver on the west and Canadian frontier points on the east, or between points intermediate thereto. Even on business, for example, from San Francisco to Canadian points, formerly wholly enjoyed by the American roads, we have no means of knowing whether the Canadian Pacific Railway obeys the law or not in this regard; for that company might take freight to Winnipeg at a higher rate than for same class of traffic through Winnipeg to Chicago; but the consignee in Canada, even if he knew our law, would be very unlikely to seek or receive redress from a United States Court or Commission as against a Canadian road.

Shippers from time to time aver, in forsaking United States lines, that one inducement to ship by the Canadian Pacific is that the published classification is closely adhered to if freight is shipped by the American lines; whereas, if they ship by the Canadian Pacific, there are no precautions against improper representations of contents of packages or under-billing. We have neither the right nor the power to test whether such allegations are well-founded or not.

I may observe, however, that the Southern Pacific Company is the receiving carrier for all east-bound, and the delivering carrier for all west-bound, overland freight transported by rail from or to San Francisco and adjacent cities in California, and as such is held to a strict accountability for proper classification and billing of freight, both by reason of its own interests and the jealousies of lines interested on the one hand, and for the due protection of the public on the other. The Canadian Pacific, on the contrary, being practically its own censor, and at the same time eager to secure traffic, would naturally not be very solicitous to detect the schemes of shippers for evading the published tariffs.

14. State generally what is the effect of competition of the Canadian Steamship Company upon American lines.

A.—The Southern Pacific Company and connections have suffered a large loss of revenue through Asiatic traffic being diverted by the Canadian Pacific steamers for transportation via Vancouver to and from points in the United States and Canada, which, before those steamers were put in operation, reached its destination by way of San Francisco.

The first Canadian Pacific steamer in competition with lines delivering at San Francisco sailed from Yokohama May 31, 1887; but, in their anxiety to make their influence felt in the commerce of the Pacific and divert the traffic from American lines, they ran a line of clippers, commencing with the bark "W. B. Flint," from Yokohama, June 20, 1886, and in that year thus diverted 7,300,000 pounds of tea to the Vancouver route. During the year 1888, nineteen steamers delivered their cargoes of tea and silk to the Canadian Pacific Railway at Vancouver, which consignments would otherwise have been forwarded through San Francisco over American roads. The traffic value of this diversion cannot be accurately determined through lack of the full details necessary for exact calculation; but it is safe to say that, merely by this diversion from San Francisco, the loss to the Southern Pacific Company and connections for the year 1888 on such east-bound business was not less than $272,000 on tea and $23,000 on silk, or a total loss for the year of say $300,000.

Further, for the year 1887, the American lines carried 19,333,524 pounds of tea; while for the season of 1888 they carried but 13,687,565 pounds, being a loss of 29 per cent.

On the other hand, during the season of 1887, the Canadian Pacific carried 9,900,962 pounds of tea, but in 1888 carried 13,582,911 pounds, being a gain of 37 per cent. Of course, every pound of tea carried by the Canadian Pacific was business which the American lines should still have enjoyed. The loss in tonnage, however, represents but partially the damage done by the competition of the Canadian lines.

The average through rate from Asia to Eastern cities on tea in 1885 was $2.97 per 100 pounds, in 1886 was $2.77, in 1887 fell to $2.08, and in 1888 was further forced down by the foreign competition to $1.73 per 100 pounds. Incidentally, it may be observed that the difference in the freight rate cannot benefit the consumer to any appreciable extent, although aggregating large losses in revenue to the American carriers.

Further, in this connection, I would call attention to the fact that, as the average through tea rate in 1885 was $2.97 per 100 pounds, Canadian Pacific competition not then existing, we may calculate that to be the rate we should have enjoyed in 1888 but for such competition, on which basis the American through lines, ocean and rail, via San Francisco, lost nearly $660,000 on the diverted tea tonnage alone. Similarly, on the raw silk shipments, American steamer and rail lines may be set down as losing no less than $46,000, or over $700,000 lost on the items of diverted tea and raw silk alone.

The American lines, too, carried this reduced tonnage at low rates under an increased operating expense, the rail lines being compelled, by the Canadian Pacific's aggressive efforts, to give the silk passenger-train service, and the tea special, fast service as against the slower but satisfactory service formerly given these commodities.

It is important to bear in mind that these figures include only tea and raw silk carried during the year 1888 on through bills of lading from Asiatic ports to Eastern cities and diverted to the Canadian Pacific line, via Vancouver, but do not include the miscellaneous merchandise diverted to that route or the tonnage carried by steamers of the Canadian line to Pacific Coast ports in the United States, all of which was formerly transported by American companies. Neither do they take into account the fact that practically all the Asiatic tonnage the American steamer lines did themselves secure in competition with the Canadian Pacific line was at greatly reduced rates owing to that competition.

As to west-bound tonnage carried by the Canadian Pacific Company from Eastern cities of the United States to Asia, we have little definite information; and we have no statistics as to the tonnage from Pacific Coast ports to Asia, diverted by the Canadian Pacific line from the Pacific Mail and Occidental and Oriental Steamship Companies' lines from San Francisco. From data furnished by the United States Inspector of Customs at Vancouver, B. C., it appears that of cotton-piece goods, or domestics alone, 5,351,668 pounds were exported from the New England States through that port during the last six months of 1888. During the twelve months preceding, which ended June 30, 1888, there were exported by that route 5,625,000 pounds of these goods. These figures indicate a rapid increase of the volume of this branch of traffic; and in confirmation of this conclusion it may be noted that during the month of January, 1889, no less than 2,400,000 pounds of these goods were similarly exported via Vancouver. As the total export of cotton goods from the United States to China during the year 1888 amounted to 31,000,000 yards, or about 10,000,000 pounds, it would therefore appear that eighty per cent of the total export of cotton goods from the United States to China during the year 1888 were shipped over the Canadian Pacific Railway and steamer lines. It is fair to assume that the Canadian Pacific's influence in the diversion of miscellaneous American manufactures is also becoming serious.

As to passenger business, the influence of the Canadian Pacific line on the passenger traffic formerly transported by American carriers can be but imperfectly determined, on account of the difficulty of obtaining statistics which convey an adequate idea of the variations in the business involved. We are unable to say to what extent ocean passenger travel between the Pacific coast and Asiatic ports, in either direction, has been diverted from the Pacific Mail and Occidental and Oriental Steamship Companies to the Vancouver route, and likewise have no data within reach to show what travel between European points and Asia, across the North American continent, has been lost to the American rail and ocean companies through the competition of the Canadian carriers.

We are able to state, however, on the authority of the Auditor of the Trans-continental Association, that there were 10,460 through passengers by way of the Canadian Pacific Railway to and from the principal cities in California, Oregon, Washington Territory and the western coast of British Columbia during the six months ending December 31, 1888.

This travel, amounting to say 21,000 passengers per annum, must have sought the American lines had this foreign competitor not been in the field.

15. What remedy, if any, do you suggest to protect American railroad and steamship lines against the competition of the Canadian Pacific road and the Canadian steamship line?

A.—The Canadian Pacific Company exists and compels recognition. It came into existence, it is true, under more favorable conditions than any other transportation line on the American continent. It is a privileged competitor against the carriers in the United States, and the reasons for this are many and exceptional. The road extends from Montreal, on the St. Lawrence, to Vancouver in British Columbia, a distance of 2,905 miles. It also has lines to Quebec and into the State of Maine, and direct connections with many of the United States roads, thus giving it entry into the principal seaport and interior cities of the United States between the Atlantic seaboard and the Missouri river. It also has direct connection with the Northwest through Winnipeg and St. Paul, connecting with several domestic roads—in all controlling a mileage of 4,960. Its road is well equipped with rolling stock of modern design and in great abundance. It runs its own steamers on the great lakes, and is now building a line to Halifax, Nova Scotia, soon to be in operation, which will give it a connection with European ports nearer by several hundred miles than any United States ports.

The Canadian Pacific road, as an individual corporation, has really been built by the Canadian Government, their gifts of money, of land and of credit being unexampled in the history of the world, not hesitating even at largely increasing the national debt to expedite the road's completion.

As already mentioned, the Canadian Pacific Railway is, under its charter, freed for all time from taxation, by the Dominion or by any Province established after the date of the charter. Its land grant in the western territory is also freed from taxation for twenty years, unless sold in the meantime.

The Canadian Pacific Railway, in consequence of the munificent aid it has received, has the lowest fixed charges of any system of roads on the American continent, being less per mile by one-half than the average fixed charges per mile of the combined United States roads for interest on their bonded debt alone. It also has cheap labor and material for its construction, repairs and maintenance expenses. It has, accessible to a large portion of its lines, extensive fields of coal of the finest quality and in exhaustless quantity, thus insuring an abundant fuel supply at low prices, in contrast with which the item of fuel alone is a most serious expense to the Southern Pacific Company, which pays a greater price therefor than any other company on this continent, the 6,000 miles of country through which its roads run being without available coal.

This much-favored foreign company should not enjoy privileges and immunities denied the railroads of the United States under the interstate commerce law, which, so far as it concerns the subject under consideration, should, as I view it, be so amended as to recognize the unequal contest in which the United States carriers are forced to engage with foreign carriers seeking United States or international traffic.

Interstate or international traffic of foreign carriers should therefore be regulated by treaty and legislation, or other adequate means. Further than this, the law should include all transportation lines—water as well as rail—competing for the traffic upon which the railroads of the United States depend for revenue to meet their financial obligations, which is of the utmost importance to the people dependent on the roads and enjoying the benefits they confer.

It has recently been announced that a grant of £60,000, or, in round figures, $300,000 per annum, has been arranged with her Britannic Majesty's Government as a postal subsidy for a line of steamers to carry the mails between Vancouver and Chinese and Japanese ports. It has been asserted also that an admiralty or secret subsidy is additionally provided for these steamers.

Compare with this the total amount paid by the United States of less than $17,000 for the carriage via San Francisco in 1888 of trans-Pacific postal mattter which was nearly thirty times heavier than that of the Canadian line. In other words, and the British Dominion Governments are contributing most liberally to the cost of maintaining a steamship line across the Pacific, just as the Dominion Government paid so bountifully towards the construction of their great military and commercial railroad line across the continent. A steamship line thus subsidized and controlled by an overland road under one management from ocean to ocean, admirably built and with a magnificent equipment far in excess of current needs, unhampered by our restrictive commerce laws, is naturally taking, gradually but surely, the traffic properly belonging to the carriers of the United States.

The Canadian Pacific Company, then, being practically exempt from our laws, can dictate the rates and most successfully compete for the trans-continental traffic, taking the same at less rates than the United States roads can afford to accept; taking it, too, without depleting the revenue natural to and necessary for its local traffic. The United States roads, on the other hand, are tied up under restrictive provisions, and are compelled to make large sacrifices of their local earnings if they would compete with the foreign lines for the through traffic. It may be said that there is no conflict apparent between the United States carriers and their Canadian competitors; but there is no conflict only because the foreign line stands in the position of a victor, for it was able to demand unreasonable concessions as the price of its co-operation with the overland roads of the United States, who had to accept the best terms they could obtain. Were that company in reality subject to the same rigid restrictions as the United States roads, it could not have enforced unreasonable demands, nor could it, in this or any other respect, be in a position to transact business within the limits of the United States under conditions more favorable than accorded to American lines. Therefore, I am of the opinion, after years of experience and observation in traffic affairs, that if any of the carriers are subjected to legislative restrictions, all the competing carriers, domestic and foreign, rail and water, should be placed under like and uniform control.

The results sought should be fair and remunerative rates for the carriers, and at the same time reasonable and stable rates for the public.

As between American rail carriers, the great obstacle (apart from foreign competition) heretofore encountered in maintaining stability of rates, is the competition of ocean and inland water carriers. These water carriers should, I believe, be made strictly amenable to the interstate commerce law, so long as that law is enforced against the railroads. It should be further made legal for the rail lines to enter with such water carriers into joint traffic arrangements for the purpose of avoiding demoralization of the transportation and commercial interests involved; the law to grant the carriers permission to pool and equitably divide their earnings on the traffic if necessary.

Having thus afforded American rail carriers a much needed and proper relief from wasteful and unjustifiable competition with each other, or with inexpensive carriers over water-ways which cost nothing to maintain, such competition being admittedly hurtful alike to the shipper and the carrier, I would then by treaty and legislation provide and enforce that the rates charged by American roads on United States or international traffic should be the minimum which the foreign competitor may accept on the same traffic, and, if needful, would permit the American lines to enter into a pool of earnings with their competitor.

Experience has demonstrated that pools protect not only the carrier, but the shipper as well; and I cannot too strongly recommend that this matter be carefully and thoroughly considered by Congress, as tending to promote the best interests of the shipper and the carrier.

Having referred briefly to the effect of the operation of the Canadian railroads and steamship companies upon the business of the United States railroads and steamship lines upon the Pacific, and the partial remedy suggested to place them more nearly on an equality in competing for through traffic with foreign lines, I would say it seems to me that the American Steamship lines are placed at such a great disadvantage that Congress, in its united wisdom, should pass a law to assist the American mercantile steam-ship lines by offering as liberal compensation for the transportation of mails as foreign Governments bestow on their carriers, and as most notedly is done by that great maritime nation of the world, Great Britain, which is rapidly encroaching upon the rights of the citizens of our Republic.

16. State any further matter which occurs to you perti-nent to the subject upon which you have been examined.

A.—I would respectfully submit to your honorable com-mittee that, while the damage already done to American transportation interests by Canadian carriers is sufficiently serious in itself, it is trifling in comparison to the damage likely to be inflicted by our Canadian competitors in the future, because of the unique position they occupy as against American carriers. Their influence on American traffic is already pronounced and conspicuous, and it would not be unnatural if, emboldened by their past success in capturing that which the American lines have built up and heretofore held, they would in future become more aggres-sive, seeing that they command the valuable local traffic of a vast domain, the earnings from which are absolutely unaffected by any rates they choose to make to secure American tonnage, however low they may deem it neces-sary to make those rates.

By its charter the Canadian Pacific Railway was given the sole right to operate or construct railroads west of Ontario. How valuable this right is deemed by that com-pany and the Dominion Government may be gleaned from the circumstance that, when the province of Manitoba revolted against that concession, so far as it was concerned, the Dominion Government, in consideration of the company relinquishing that provision of its franchise for a portion of Manitoba, guaranteed the interest at three and a half per cent on bonds amounting to $15,000,000, payable in fifty years. The Canadian Pacific, through this provision of its charter, stands without danger of a rival west of Ontario for twenty years.

The total expenditure by the Dominion Government on the Canadian Pacific Railway to June 30, 1887, was over $60,000,000, in itself an unparalleled endowment, independently of the extraordinary franchise and lavish grants of land bestowed on that company. The splendor of these concessions must not cause us to overlook other privileges most important in the construction and maintenance of a trans-continental railway, such as importation duty free of steel rails and other material used in construction of the rail and telegraph line, and freedom of the railway from taxation forever.

Contrast with this the conditions under which the American roads exist—the transcontinental lines competing not only with each other and with the ocean lines in endeavoring to secure overland traffic, but being compelled to compete also against that foreign line which has no vital interest or tangible responsibility dependent on its conduct of American traffic. Even were its through and local business interdependent and subject to the control of our Government, as in the case of American lines, it should be observed that the fixed charges for interest on the funded debt of the Canadian Pacific Railway averaged $655.28 per mile, according to poor's Manual for 1888; whereas the average interest on the funded debt alone of the combined railroads of the United States is, according to the same authority, $1,332.46 per mile, and the average taxes (per last United States census) of those railroads $151.33 per mile, making a total of $1,483.79 per mile. Thus the fixed charges per mile of the Canadian Railway in these particulars are but 44 per cent of like charges to be met by the United States roads. It will be noticed, therefore, that to meet vital financial obligations—the failure to do which would be disastrous alike to the railroads and the general public, and would admittingly be against public policy—it is necessary that the American roads earn $2.25 per mile for each dollar the Canadian Pacific is required to earn. In the general average thus given for the combined roads in the United States, the vast and inexpensive mileage of the roads constructed in the great plains and valleys of the East is included with the smaller mileage of the roads west of the Missouri river, constructed through mountainous and comparatively sparsely settled districts where the cost of construction and maintenance is high; and I may add that it is upon the latter the great burden of conflict with our Canadian Pacific competitor falls.

While referring to these latter roads, I would call your attention to the great contrast between the privilege granted the Canadian Pacific of importing their material duty free, and the restrictions laid on the Central Pacific Railroad, for example, which was built under the eye of this Government and was expressly restrained from availing itself of the cheaper markets of the world. It could not buy its iron or rails in Wales or Belgium; it could not ship its material to San Francisco under a foreign flag; it was forced to purchase American rails at an average of over $80 per ton, while foreign rails could be purchased at an average, including duty, of $50 per ton; it was forced to pay $17.50 per ton for freight from New York to San Francisco, when it could have shipped from Cardiff to San Francisco for less than $10; it was forced to pay a war insurance for freight thus shipped under the American flag as high as 17 per cent, when the same goods could have floated under the English flag for less than 3 per cent. On many locomotives it purchased there was a war tax paid to the Government of $960 each.

What wonder, then, that this company and other Amercan lines, all dependent on their earning power for capacity to meet their financial obligations, should view with misgiving, not to say with alarm, the encouragement of their Canadian rival, which has been indulgently nursed into vigorous life by a foreign Government, and whose object is, by the use of Government subsidies on land and sea, to divert American commerce from American ocean and rail transportation lines; nor are the transportation lines alone interested. This diversion affects every seaport from which the business is diverted, and every town and city which the traffic ceases to traverse when diverted to Canadian lines. It cannot even be said in mitigation that consumers are benefited by the diversion; for it is obvious that, except on raw materials, the cost of transportation enters but slightly into the price the consumer pays for any commodity; while on articles of general consumption the cost of transportation is almost, if not altogether, imperceptible.

Therefore it would seem to be the first duty of this Government to adopt such measures as may be necessary to protect and foster its own vast and important commercial interests, no longer indulging the apathy which is so well calculated to further the ambitious schemes of our foreign neighbors, who are striving to wrest from us commerce rightfully our own.

SUPPLEMENTAL.

The liberty you gave me in your sixteenth inquiry regarding our relations with Canada, "State any further matter which occurs to you pertinent to the subject upon which you have been examined," prompts me to supplement the foregoing answers with some observations, reflections and suggestions. I do this with the assurance of your permission and the hope that you will pardon me for further reference to the subject of rail and waterways in the United States and their relations with those of Canada.

That the United States, under a system protective of our industries, has prospered in a greater degree than the people of any other time or nation is universally conceded. Great Britain, on the other hand, largely depending for her prosperity, as a free-trader, on a share in the commerce of the world, was thwarted in her designs and hopes by the result of our last election, which decided the issue that seemed so threatening to our commerce and industries, and finally settled the future policy of the United States. By voice of the people, PROTECTION was the banner to be hung upon the outer walls, and which was unfurled on the East, South and West ; but on the North, forsooth, the greatest of commercial powers is left free to prey upon our border and enjoy the fruits of a policy calculated to enrich its people and Government at the expense of our own. I refer to the result of the election not in a partisan spirit, but merely as illustrating the temper of the American people on the subject.

CANADIAN PACIFIC RAILWAY INIMICAL TO AMERICAN INTERESTS.

The most subtile instance of England's movements for the maintenance of commercial supremacy, the invasion of American commerce, and the absorption of the benefits of American prosperity, is found in the Canadian Pacific Railway and its steamship lines. Not only has this road, with its cheap construction and equipment, its cheap labor and bounteous Government assistance, already cut largely into a carrying trade that rightfully belongs to the United States, but it is steadily reaching forth to seize more.

The President of the Canadian Pacific Railway is reported to have said that his company was getting, at the present time, about ten per cent of the entire trans-continental traffic. Since this gentleman is reported to have admitted that this amount represented only about four per cent of the entire traffic of his company, it is evident that this great subsidized and foreign corporation can afford to force the rates down far below the cost of carriage, thus dictating the rates at which the roads of the United States must accept the remaining ninety per cent of the traffic — naturally theirs — or abandon the business. Ten per cent of the traffic may not seem large to the casual observer; but it should not be forgotten that the taking of a tenth at a non-paying rate would of itself do little or no harm to that company—not burdened with as heavy responsibilities as the American trans-continental lines and having a valuable local business ; but it fixes the rates for, say, one-third of the entire traffic of competing American lines at which they must accept the business or surrender to the foreign carrier, which pays out no money to our people, owes no allegiance to this country, and of course is not compelled to respect the strict and binding laws enforced upon the American carriers.

This impending danger to our industries and enterprise and this curious feature of protection, which has not yet attracted the attention it merits, should engage the earnest consideration of Congress.

We have before us, too, the example of our mercantile marine, wherein it will be found that in 1855, American vessels carried 75½ per cent of our exports and imports, while in 1861 we carried but 66½ per cent ; after the ordeal of the civil war in 1865 we carried but 28 per cent, and for the fiscal year ending June 30th, 1888, something less than 14 per cent. This decline of the American foreign carrying trade has occurred, too, in the face of a marvelous growth in our foreign commerce, and hence leads to the inevitable conclusion that foreign vessels have taken the traffic from us. Proof that they have is to be found in the fact that our ship-building for the foreign carrying trade has likewise steadily declined "until in the fiscal year ending June 30th, 1888," to use the language of the Hon. Nelson Dingley, Jr., member of Congress from Maine, in an able paper on this subject: "there was not one ship, and but few other vessels, built in this country for the foreign trade." This result has been brought about by placing our ships in unequal competition with their British rivals, which, constructed where money is cheap, where coal and iron are procured at a minimum expense, and skilled artisans receive but meager remuneration for their labor, can be launched at a cost far below ours, and are then manned by officers and seamen whose scale of compensation ranges low. Thus in operation under advantages not enjoyed by our vessels, they further receive financial aid from their Government whereever new commerce is sought to be developed, or it is seen that competition can be broken down. Our ships, on the other hand, are more expensive carriers by reason of the higher cost of all that enters into their construction and operation, chief among which is the higher cost of American labor, whose wages we should seek to maintain in the interest of universal prosperity. The hesitancy of our Government toward aiding any private or quasi private enterprises has further handicapped us by depriving American ships of the financial aid Great Britain is accustomed to render her carriers and ship-builders. As a natural consequence of such unequal conditions, the American foreign carrying trade has become diverted almost wholly from American to foreign vessels. What a happy contrast is presented by our domestic shipping, which has prospered during the very period our foreign carrying trade steadily declined. The cause is not far to seek. Our navigation laws restrict our domestic commerce to American vessels, which, thus protected from unequal competition with foreign carriers, occupy their natural sphere with profit to themselves and benefit to the people. Since the charges for such transportation but remotely affect the consumer, and in articles of consumption are imperceptible to them, it follows that the small additional fraction American craft might charge would be unnoticed and insignificant to the people while constituting to the carriers the difference between working at a profit or being driven out of the trade. How different had been the fate of our domestic shipping if left to struggle against the competition of foreign craft, is not a matter of idle conjecture but of knowledge founded, as we have seen, on sad experience.

Apply the same principles to the transportation of American traffic by rail as have thus affected the American shipping trade, and like results may reasonably be looked for. Introduce the competition of foreign railroad lines constructed under signally favorable conditions which, for example, render it needful for them to earn but one dollar to meet their fixed charges where the average American road has to earn two dollars and twenty-five cents;* operating under lax responsibilities which permit them, if they please, to carry trans-continental traffic from State to State of our nation at rates below the cost of carriage, without perceptibly affecting their finances; enable them to continue this until they practically drive the American roads out of the through business, and it

---

* See my answer to Question 16 of Senate Committee.

will be seen, when perhaps it is too late, that foreign enterprise has been nurtured at the expense and by the sacrifice of American interests. Our navigation laws restrict our domestic commerce to American vessels. Why should our laws not proceed on the same lines to restrict our domestic railway transportation to American rail carriers? Who can contend that American prosperity has been furthered by the ruinous competition to which our merchant marine in the foreign trade has succumbed? Or who will contend that our prosperity has been checked by preserving our domestic water transportation for American vessels? As futile is it to argue that in railway transportation unequal competition benefits American˗ interests, or contrariwise that the protection of American railways against foreign aggression will be a hindrance to the prosperity of the American nation.

The Protective System should Apply to Transportation.

According to the last census report (1880), the capital invested in manufactures (including petroleum refining, mining industries and fisheries, but not including value of product of hand trades, as carpenters, masons, blacksmiths, and others working singly, or the statistics of gas manufacturing or manufacturing by steam railroads, which two industries last named are not summarized in copy of census reports at hand) was $2,817,598,352
Number of hands employed 3,108,118
Total wages paid during the year . . . . . $ 952,335,367
Value of products $5,430,821,082

Capital invested and total wages paid in mining industries and fisheries are also omitted from the census reports; but this amount, whatever it may be, is probably so small as not to materially affect any comparisons.

According to reliable estimates, the total railroad mileage in the United States at the end of the year 1888 was about 154,000 miles, and the number of railroad adult employés is probably not less than 850,000, representing a population of nearly six millions, one-tenth the entire inhabitants of the United States, who are entitled to protection. But as no reliable statistics, either for manufactures or railroad operations, appear to be available for the years 1887 or 1888, we will confine the comparisons to 1880. In 1880, then, the total number of miles of road in the United States, according to the last census report, was 87,701 miles; the total cost of these roads was as follows:

Construction of road $4,112,367,175
Equipment 418,045,458
Lands 103,319,845
Telegraph lines and miscellaneous . . 204,913,195

Total $4,838,645,673

The gross earnings for the year 1880 were $580,450,594; operating expenses, not including interest on invested capital, $352,800,120.

It will be noticed that general manufacturing, requiring an investment of less than $3,000,000,000 of capital, turned out products to the total value of nearly $5,500,000,000, nearly all of which is moved by the railways; while, on the other hand, nearly $5,000,000,000 of capital invested in railroads produced as gross earnings from that of which they have to sell, viz., TRANSPORTATION, less than $600,000,000. It will further be noticed that there was 71.7 per cent more capital invested in railroads (no less important to the interests of the country) than in manufacturing operations for the year 1880; and it is probable this percentage is very considerably larger at the present time, as undoubtedly the investment of capital in railroads has been proportionately much greater than similar investments in manufacturing industries. These wage-earners in the railroad service, as well as the shareholders and the purchasers of our railroad securities, are as much entitled to adequate protection as are the workers in, and owners of, other property in whatsoever form. Grant protection to the manufacturer and the producer, and it must, on similar equitable grounds, be extended to the railway interest. While all else is or has been protected against undue foreign competition, the railroad industry—one of the foremost of the country—railroad capital, railroad investment and all railroad interests have been not only ignored but put as it were, under a ban, and made the victim of a system which the railroads themselves have been so often accused of pursuing, to wit:

UNJUST DISCRIMINATION.

Such discrimination consists in this: That while all other industries are encouraged and protected against foreign competition, railroad enterprises are hampered by unwise and prejudiced legislation, too often instigated by a false and ill-advised public clamor. Hence we find our great system of trans-continental railways forced into an unequal competition with a foreign system. And forced by what? Not by the natural advantages of our rival, but by arbitrary and oppressive legislation by our own people,—legislation which could not have been more effective to this end if actually conceived and executed in behalf of our Canadian competitor. This competitor meanwhile is not only necessarily free and in reality untrammeled of Governmental supervision and action, but is fostered, subsidized, aided and financially indorsed by its Government in all its efforts to wrest away

American commerce. The American transportation companies competing with it are under Governmental control and severe regulation, which seriously impair their ability to resist the foreign aggression. This Governmental control is not only exercised by the Federal Government, but it is claimed and pursued by the States of our Union, by the counties of the States and the municipalities within the counties, thus subjecting the railway corporation to four separate and distinct powers of regulation. Such injurious regulation not only affects the invested capital, but reacts on the people at large by needlessly interfering with the public usefulness of such corporations.

THE "LONG AND SHORT HAUL CLAUSE" OF THE INTERSTATE COMMERCE LAW SHOULD BE REPEALED.

If in connection with this subject I should be asked to suggest a method for improving the position of American railroads in their competition with foreign carriers, I would as a first step point to the Interstate Commerce Law and would do so not as a captious critic, impatient of Governmental control,—for while it is the law of the land I shall yield to no one in the desire to faithfully follow its spirit,— but as one whose life has been spent in the handling of railway transportation and the practical rather than theoretical solution of railway problems.

It is not to be wondered at that this Government, in its initial attempt to regulate our internal railway communication, and basing that attempt for the most part on foreign models of very limited application, should further unintentionally complicate the relations, already delicate, between the people and the carriers. All practical railway students foresaw that some of the theories embodied in the regulating law must prove a barrier to the more extended usefulness of the roads as public servants; and, the law having now received a fair trial, it has become the settled belief of the great majority of railroad managers and economists, concurred in by well-known commercial men of broad experience and ripe judgment, that at least one section of the Interstate Commerce Law can be materially modified without endangering or embarrasing any interest. Indeed, it becomes a grave question whether the greatest good to all would not be best subserved by its elimination from the law. That section is the fourth of the act, and is commonly known as the "Long and Short Haul Clause." It cannot be disputed that uniformity of regulation, without corresponding uniformity of condition, will necessarily be a failure because founded on a fallacy, since all just regulation must have reference to the condition which makes it necessary or advisable. Completely or even approximatety analogous conditions cannot exist over the wide area of our country, which, although under the same Government, presents contrasting and sometimes perplexing physical characteristics, with resources and products as varied as might be found in the combined area of many empires. Governmental regulation, to be efficient, must therefore be so readily adaptable that the reason claimed as calling forth the regulation shall have complete justification in the condition to which such regulation is addressed.

This Interstate question was before Congress and under discussion some nine years. The movement was started the year following the well-known decision of the U. S. Supreme Court, in the "Granger" cases. The agitation grew out of the anti-railroad craze of those days, from which such State enactments as the *Potter Law* resulted, under which trade was so much disturbed and perplexed as to compel its repeal after a short trial. Early anti-railroad extremists did not find an easy solution of the complicated questions of railroad policy. They passed laws without regard to commercial results; and contrasts were never more manifest between theory and practice than between the provisions of those laws and the facts which enter into the business principles of railroad management.

Following in this line of political tradition, it is not strange that Congress, in its attempt at regulation,—guided by the light of previous experiments of very limited range and by the information gleaned from the inadequate testimony of railroad officials whose experience was connected with the old thickly settled and rich manufacturing sections of the country, with but slight regard to the South and the vast territory west of the Mississippi,—should pass a law not wholly practicable or adapted to the dissimilar circumstances and varied conditions surrounding railroad operation in the different sections of the country.

The tariffs in existence at the time the Interstate Law took effect, covering all the railroads and water-ways, were not the result of mere guesswork, but came from two generations of experience and actual practice, and were of natural growth, being devised to bring the producer and consumer together, to their mutual advantage, however distant they might be. Considering this work from a national standpoint, railroad rates were thus reduced to a figure unequaled elsewhere, stimulating the most wonderful national development mankind has ever known.

The traffic managers, in making their schedules, which were accompanied by such satisfactory results, found that the country was so large, its topography and resources so varied, its commercial relations so complex, and the railroad interests generally so diversified, that to arbitrarily measure and bind them by rules which in practice would be found fixed and unyielding, must seriously impair the public usefulness of railway operations. These traffic officers, by business training

and the comprehensive information derived from long
experience, understand the laws and currents of our
trade and commerce; thoroughly acquainted with the
resources tributary to their respective lines and their
relation to the general weal, it has naturally ever been
their aim to adopt such a basis for their rate schedules
as would best attain those prime objects of railway construction and sound operation : first, the acquisition of
earnings large enough to adequately remunerate the capital
invested; and second, to that end the fullest natural development of all resources tributary to the road, and
without which it could not subsist and prosper. *These
two objects, it should be borne in mind, are interdependent and always uppermost in the minds of railway
managers,* however the difficulties of the multifarious
problems to be solved by them may sometimes obscure
those objects from the superficial observer. It is, we
believe, the popular failure to perceive this potent but
subtle fact that leads to legislation of the kind embodied
in the fourth section of the Interstate Commerce Law,
which provides that under substantially similar conditions
it shall be unlawful for a carrier to charge or receive any
greater compensation in the aggregate for transportation
for a shorter than for a longer distance over the same line
in the same direction. The word "substantially," as used
in the law, is, I may observe, most delusive, and in the
construction so far placed upon it, renders it a matter of
the utmost hazard, under severe civil and criminal penal-
ties, for rail carriers to construe the fourth clause as other
than an absolute inhibition, except when such an im-
periously constraining force as Cape Horn competition
between the Atlantic and Pacific Coasts controls their
action.

The fourth section of the law does violence to the very
basis, fiscal and commercial, of the railway system of the
country, seeking to displace by an arbitrary theory the

results of practical experience, which have so well met the needs of the widely diversified growth of our great Republic. Were the maintenance of this section accompanied by any tangible advantages to the business world, to compensate for its disturbing and needlessly restrictive functions, I could watch with less misgiving what developments might come. On the contrary, however, I feel bound to say that its theory is mischievous, the expression of its intent obscure, and its practical tendency is to impede American railroads in their efforts to retain American traffic as against their Canadian rivals. Further than this, it checks railway enterprise in reaching out for new markets in the interest of commerce, a check in itself hurtful as much to the public as to the railroads.

THE LAW SHOULD AUTHORIZE RAILROAD CO-OPERATION.

There is another matter of great importance regarding which I would suggest a change, if I should be asked for a further method of improving the position of American railroads. The fifth section of the Interstate Commerce Law provides :

"That it shall be unlawful for any common carrier "subject to the provisions of this act to enter into any "contract, agreement or combination with any other com- "mon carrier or carriers for the pooling of freights of "different and competing railroads, or to divide between "them the aggregate or net proceeds of the earnings of "such railroads, or any portion thereof."

Experience has shown that, when the word "pool" was introduced into railroad parlance, a great mistake was made; for the public, careless of distinctions in a subject with which they are but slightly acquainted, at once surmised that a railway pool had some sort of affinity with a pool in stocks or a pool on a race track, wherein mystery, chance and deceit were to be expected and were usual accessories. The railway pool has about it nothing of mystery or chance, but is a plain and candid business understanding between rival transportation companies, having for its purpose the prevention of such extreme competition as is ruinous to the railroads and at the same time is a public danger. *The pool is intended only to regulate competition.* The very basis according to which the earnings of the pooled roads are apportioned should indicate that the pool is not intended to stop competition. This basis is, that parallel or connecting and competing roads shall determine among themselves, or, failing in that, shall decide through skilled arbitrators what percentage of the total tonnage or earnings each of the carriers, operating in a certain defined territory, would be likely to secure at fair and steady rates, but in the absence of unjust discriminations which, in some forms or other, are always the outgrowth of unrestricted competition. The percentage determined represents the share of the traffic the respective carriers shall be awarded during a period of the future as may be decided. Each company, it is true, receives into its treasury the earnings from the traffic it carries during the period for which the apportionment was made ; but, as soon as the pool accounts can be balanced, an adjustment is made between the parties by payment of equalizing balances, less perhaps a certain portion of the surplus earnings, which, by agreement, may be retained by the disbursing company to cover the cash outlay incurred in moving the surplus traffic. The leading factor in thus apportioning the business among the lines interested is what is aptly known as "the record of the past ;" the proportion each carrier should have being assumed to be that proportion of the total traffic in question which it secured during a given previous period as against the others pooling. The next factor is a consideration of the extent to which the amount of traffic secured by each, during the basing period, was influenced by unequal rates or unfair devices. Preferential rates or devices for favored shippers cannot exist under an effective pool ; and, if any carrier has been using such to divert business to its line, this fact weighs against it. Another factor is the influence for injury of each party relatively to the other or to all ; for a carrier unable to secure any but an insignificant proportion of the traffic if compelled to use fair or equal rates, and having at the best but a small interest in traffic of great importance to other lines, could utterly demoralize the business of all lines by simply cutting the rates to a non-paying figure until it compelled a recognition of its power to inflict damage.

I have said the *leading* factor is the "record of the past." This is true, not of the initial apportionment of the traffic only, but is at the foundation of the whole fabric ; for the pool agreement always makes provision for a change in the percentages of apportionment from time to time, and these changes are based on the same considerations as at the outset. The operation of the pool modifies that factor in adjustment to which I have alluded, namely, the influence of unequal and unfair rates and preferential devices, and brings into still more prominent consideration "the record of the past." Every subsequent apportionment must of necessity be based on the traffic carried, and the conditions under which carried, by each party to the pool. It can readily be seen, therefore, that the more steadily the pool is maintained, and the longer its duration, the more strongly must the record of what each member has so far accomplished in securing business come into prominence as the leading consideration in such apportionment. Finally, indeed, the obnoxious factor referred to must disappear as the incentive to its continuance is removed. Then the carrier that is best equipped, has the best facilities, whose line is the most attractive, and has the best organization,—that can, in short, give *the best value for the money* and has the best method for inducing travel and securing traffic, is the one that will maintain its lead, as it naturally should and as it would under competitive conditions in any other business.

I trust I have made it clear that when transportation companies thus co-operate, the competitive principle is still maintained. The competition it is sought to obviate is only that kind which is ruinous to railroad interests, and in the light of all experience is nothing less than folly. In mercantile operations the conditions are so elastic that competition is rather healthy than injurious ; although even the courts have frequently recognized the right of mercantile co-operation when it is limited to the purpose of holding competition within such bounds as to prevent disastrous consequences. In mercantile enterprises the investment is not fixed, the capital employed is variable, the expenses nicely adjusted to the fluctuating requirements of the establishment ; if one branch of the business is unremunerative, it can be abandoned and the capital turned into more profitable branches or perhaps into new channels. Reckless competition in any commercial sphere ends in the extinction of the weakest, and the victory of the strong. With railroads it is not so. A railroad has but one branch of business in which to operate, namely, Transportation. Its capital is sunk in the railroad property, and cannot be withdrawn to seek more paying investment, although its *value* can be reduced, and indeed utterly destroyed, to the injury of every one connected with the road or its interests. The larger part of its expenses are fixed and do not fluctuate with the volume of traffic or earnings. If it cannot earn enough to pay its fixed charges over and above the expenses of actual operation,— which in themselves aggregate very large amounts on any important railroad, and are in the main to directly compensate labor,—then there remains but one recourse, namely, *bankruptcy for the road.* This bankrupt concern does not then go out of the business of transportation, but continues in it, and with its greater financial responsibilities repudiated becomes a standing menace to every competing road struggling to fulfill its obligations. Thus the *value* of the property of one road being destroyed, every road that is drawn into competition with the wrecked concern is threatened with like destruction thereby. The weak thus becomes the strong, and the reverse of mercantile conditions results. Should the bankrupt corporation fall into the hands of stock gamblers or railroad wreckers, competing roads become the victims of their machinations, and properties once solvent succumb to dishonest and disastrous competition. Any man of business can perceive the force of this argument. To realize it he has but to ponder on the prospects of his own success in a business in which he would be forced to compete, and for an indefinite period, with bankrupt concerns of equal magnitude permitted to continue doing business on the same street and in the same block.

I am satisfied, that just as soon as this subject is popularly understood, the spirit of justice and fair play inherent in American character will manifest itself in a ready assent to the legalization of pooling, and the consequent modification of the fifth section of the law. No serious injury can be permitted to any interest of the nation as vast as that of the railroads, without reacting injuriously on the public credit; and if railroad property cannot be reasonably protected and railroad investments be equally secure as in other enterprises, the result must be, sooner or later, a stagnation in railroad building such as has already become marked in some of the States where railroads are "regulated to death." All our experience as a people, however, should teach us that to stimulate the extension of railroads into new fields is the proper and paying policy.

"Railroad War" Is Not Railroad Competition.

I have shown that when railroads are in a pool the competitive principle is still maintained, and going farther than this feel safe in asserting that the true competitive principle is maintained more thoroughly and healthfully under such regulation than when each carrier acts on its own behalf, becoming a "free lance" when it pleases, and undertaking reprisals for real or fancied wrongs.

The popular ideal of railroad competition is "railroad war;" as when, for instance, in 1886, all lines between St. Paul, Chicago, St. Louis and New Orleans on the one hand, and the Pacific Coast on the other, were struggling for supremacy in the trade interchanged between the Pacific Slope and Eastern cities; or, as when more recently, the Canadian Pacific Railway declared its intention of striving with American lines for the same traffic, and straightway proceeded to make good its avowal by cutting rates below anything the Americans attempted in endeavoring to retain the traffic developed and heretofore enjoyed by them.

What have been the results in both cases? In the former, after months of reckless warfare, during which the most conservative roads were driven, in sheer self-defense, to meet the viciously low rates of reckless competitors, a truce was patched up and efforts made to resume normal conditions. This was not done until millions of dollars had been wasted; yet a calm survey of the field shows that none of the roads gained anything, even in prestige, by the waste of resources ; and this notwithstanding what might be termed heroic sacrifices by the combatants, tonnage being sought absolutely regardless of the compensation. To cite one instance of the latter, I may mention that many carloads of Eastern goods were brought into California at rates which allowed the line hauling them only *three cents* per hundred pounds for the service Kansas City to San Francisco! Under such conditions railway interests became demoralized, commercial transactions developed in many cases into mere gambling on railroad rates; shippers were not less demoralized than the carriers; and inequalities, discriminations, mutual distrust and universal uncertainty pervaded all transactions in which transportation cut an important or perceptible figure, direct or indirect. The vicious public policy of such ordeals is well recognized ; while, so far as the carriers are concerned, the process has been aptly called "railroad assassination." In the case of the Canadian Pacific's declaration of hostilities and its acts in pursuance of it, the disaster was only less widespread because American roads hesitated to engage in conflict with a rival having all to gain and nothing to lose by the venture ; which, backed by an empire, reached out as a matter of national pride and national aggrandizement for new business to which it had no right.

I respectfully submit that in neither of these instances, from actual experience, can there be found the principle of true competition.

To make the case still plainer, I will suppose, merely by way of illustration (what may in fact occur at any time in any portion of the country), that two existing roads between well-known competing points become entangled in misunderstandings which keenly develop this so-called competition. I will take the liberty of citing New Orleans and Galveston, on the one hand, and El Paso, Texas, on the other,—El Paso being one of our commercial gateways to Mexico,—between which cities run two rail lines that actively canvass for business in competition with each other. Happily both properties are conservatively managed ; but suppose, to suit our purpose in illustration, their interests should seem to clash and their misunderstanding involve them in what is popularly termed a "war." The rates to El Paso would immediately be cut down on business from both Gulf cities, and while the latter were thus situated, the merchants of St. Louis, Kansas City and Chicago would be unable to sell their wares in El Paso because of the discrimination in favor of those at New Orleans and Galveston through the cut in rates. Impelled by the entreaties of their patrons, eager to maintain their standing in that market, the roads from the Northern cities must cut their rates to meet those from the cities in the South. Similarly the California shippers, and the anxiety of their rail line to maintain the status of California in that market, would force a cut in rates from the Pacific Coast to El Paso. Thus at a glance it will be seen that a matter which merely concerned two roads within a limited area has, through their unrestricted power for harm in case of conflict, disturbed the commercial equilibrium of all cities competing for the trade in question, and has led to sacrifice of the revenues of railroad lines having no direct interest whatever in the initial cause of the trouble. Further, if it is borne in mind that every cut in rates thus made would, under the "long and short haul clause," affect rates from or to intermediate points, the extent of the damage inflicted is made more clear. If the struggle continues, the irritation must become more intense and extended ; and as rates between Eastern cities and the Pacific Slope, for example, cannot exceed the sum of the local rates, the whole Trans-continental traffic of the country may readily become demoralized.

Perhaps I should make this plainer. The rate on any commodity moving from New Orleans, for instance, to San

Francisco, cannot, in practice or under the law, exceed the rate from New Orleans to El Paso added to the rate from El Paso to San Francisco. When rates between New Orleans and El Paso, and at the same time those between El Paso and San Francisco, are cut below a certain limit, it is manifest that rates between New Orleans and San Francisco become affected; similarly the rates between Kansas City, St. Louis and Chicago, on the one hand, and the Pacific Slope, on the other, are drawn into the struggle; and as the merchants of Omaha and St. Paul will not stand idly by and see Kansas City and St. Louis control California business merely because the rates via El Paso are shattered, they too will be forced into the wasteful struggle.

I risk your patience by thus going into detail because I want to make the conclusion clear, that railroad wars are not in the nature of true competition. In the assumed instance before us, the only competition involved was that between New Orleans and Galveston on the one hand, and El Paso on the other, or somewhere between these points, directly affecting only the interests of the two lines between which I have supposed the trouble to arise. Notwithstanding this fact, the action of the road which in such a situation should precipitate a conflict might, as we have seen, embroil the whole country, demoralizing trade and dissipating railroad earnings, and all from causes beyond the control of the victims. This is not railroad competition; it does not spring from excessive railroad rates or through any fault of the railroads thus made needlessly to suffer by the acts of other lines in localities perhaps remote. *The railroads are but the servitors of the cities with whose interests they are directly connected, and identify themselves with the public welfare by becoming the equalizing medium for maintaining the commercial standing of those cities.* When the fray is ended and the field surveyed, it is always found that the relative

position of all has remained unchanged, each locality
having found it necessary to struggle with the aim of holding its own, fortunate if it has achieved even that.
Railroad competition is one thing, railroad disaster springing
from such causes as I have assumed to illustrate is quite
another; and it is such follies I would seek to regulate.

RAILROAD CO-OPERATION CONDUCIVE TO MAINTENANCE OF NORMAL COMMERCIAL CONDITIONS.

For this feverish, spasmodic, speculative and dangerous
thing to which the name of railroad competition has been
thoughtlessly applied, I would substitute tariffs determined
after careful consideration of the needs of the shipper and
the way the railroads can most fully and fairly meet them.
Such tariffs, I would urge, can be more satisfactorily adjusted when the carriers co-operate, than under any other
conditions.

With strife rampant, a tariff becomes merely a maximum
to cut from, a foundation for improper discrimination, a
schedule of charges to be levied on the innocent and
unwary, but likely to be evaded in its application to the
shrewd or large and influential shipper. Under the pooling system, on the contrary, it ceases to be all-important
that the business be taken from the rival road even at
the cost of "cutting rates to the bottom;" it ceases to be
important that the merchant spend his days in "shop-
ping" for a low rate and urging the competing roads to
further reductions each below the other, in the hope of scor-
ing a victory by securing the coveted tonnage. It is,
instead, all important that as business has to be secured
under open and stable rates, each road shall be operated
with an eye to rendering the most efficient service in further-
ance of its own interests; and it is of ever-increasing
importance that the tariff rates under which the business

is sought shall be so constructed as to stimulate the movement of traffic, that the roads may enjoy that steadily increasing revenue for which they can only reasonably hope through healthy commercial conditions, when they shall receive and render value for value, in just recompense for services performed. Thus properly stimulated to advance their own interests by careful consideration of their patrons' needs, they are in another direction properly restrained by the most powerful influences which can be brought to bear on railroad managers, namely, the ineffaceable competition of water-ways,—which, however it may be checked, can never be broken down,—and the mighty voice of public opinion. Regarding the latter, a well-known writer* of recognized experience justly remarks :

"The restraining force of public opinion, and respect "for the common and statute law, operate upon railway "traffic management with more power than is popularly "known or believed. Railways dislike to create public "issues as to their charges, and do much more to avoid "than stimulate them ; and I refer in confirmation of this "averment to every State Railway Commission in the "Union. Railways co-operate with and concede to them "far more than they antagonize or dissent from them."

In this reflection every one having experience in railroad management will fully concur; and I believe the experience of the Interstate Commerce Commission will further sustain it.

RAILROAD CO-OPERATION vs. COMBINED OWNERSHIP.

It is unfortunate that the public mind confounds railway co-operation in pools with joint railway ownership; whereas the difference between the two relations is wide and important. A recent writer has pointed out

---

* G. R. Blanchard, on "Traffic Unity," 1894.

that the distinction is : A pooling arrangement between railroads is merely an administrative union within
well-defined bounds ; while combined ownership means
organic and fiscal union. Under a pool, each road remains
invested with its responsibilities ; its organization is not
disturbed ; it has to maintain, and, if possible, increase its
earnings, and has to do so on a fair basis, without resort
to unfair discriminations and covert devices ; it has, in
short, every incentive to develop to the utmost all the
traffic that prudent management can see its way to handling at fair rates ; and, by fair rates, I mean rates fair alike
to the shipper and the carrier. Rightly or wrongly, the
public apprehends some hidden danger from the combination of ownerships in railroad properties, unmindful
that all such combinations of any extent in the past have
resulted in an increase of facilities and a reduction in the
cost of transportation. It is at least an anomaly that those
who view with misgiving the reaction in favor of extend-
ing and combining railroad ownership should, at the same
time, prohibit competing carriers from adopting the only
method yet devised to protect themselves from destructive
conditions, while yet maintaining their separate identity
and responsibilities.

REFLECTIONS OF HON. THOMAS M. COOLEY.

In venturing thus to address you at such length on this
broad subject, I derive much encouragement and hope
from the reflection, that in my convictions I am generally
sustained by no less an authority on affairs pertaining to
transportation and its administration than the Honorable
Thos. M. Cooley, Chairman of the Interstate Commerce
Commission, over whose signature was published in the
Chicago Railway Review of April 26, 1884, a paper entitled " Popular and Legal Views of Traffic Pooling,"

which is a most able and pithy exposition of the topic. I cannot refrain from quoting his concluding remarks, replete with profound and significant suggestion :

" That the railroad problem, so far as it is involved in
" wars of rates between the roads, cannot as yet be consid-
" ered solved, is very manifest ; the railroad companies
" have only made an effort in the direction of solving it.
" Common agreements, if they had the encouragement
" and protection of the law, would very probably supply
" it ; but for that purpose legislation would seem to be
" essential; but legislation would be mischievous rather
" than beneficial, unless it was conceived in the spirit of
" statesmen, and was made to express neither special
" favor for, nor special hostility to, the interest it would
" regulate. The railroad interest of this country repre-
" sents an enormous aggregate of wealth, and an increas-
" ing aggregate of corporate poverty; and it has immense
" capabilities for good or evil to the people. It can-
" not possibly be for the interest of any country that
" so large a proportion of the invested capital should
" be wasted or unremunerative, especially when in that
" condition its necessary tendency is to favor dishonest
" management and gambling speculation. On the other
" hand, it is for the interest of the country that the public
" shall receive, in as large a degree as shall be possible, the
" benefits which were calculated upon in providing
" by law for the building of the roads. Regulating
" legislation, should therefore, be conceived neither
" exclusively in the interest of railroad companies
" nor in the spirit of hostility to them. What the country
" needs is that they shall be made useful; not that they
" shall be crippled or bankrupted, or made stock-jobbing
" conveniences for their managers. And, no doubt, when
" the whole subject is carefully examined and wisely con-
" sidered, it will be found that the true interests of the

"owners of railroad property may be used to harmonize
"perfectly with the true interests of the public, and that
"it will be as wise for the State to encourage and protect
"whatever in corporate arrangements is of beneficial ten-
"dency as it will to suppress what is mischievous."

SUGGESTED CHANGES IN THE LAW.

I would accordingly respectfully urge on your Honorable
body that our relations with Canada render proper and
just a suggestion that Congress revoke the provision of the
law which prohibits pooling, and thereby deprives
American carriers of one means of defense against their
Canadian rival, as indicated in my answer to your 15th
interrogatory. Even in the event of legislation on the
lines so clearly laid down in the language I have quoted
from the Hon. Thos. M. Cooley, who was at that time
Justice of the Supreme Court of Michigan, and Professor
of Constitutional Law in the University of that State, I
believe the interests of the people as well as the railroads
could be fully protected by placing the pooling organizations under the scrutiny of the Interstate Commerce
Commission, who could exercise like regulative functions
in reference thereto as now delegated to them by Congress in matters pertaining to interstate traffic. Finally,
I believe such organizations would greatly facilitate the
administration of the Interstate Commerce Law and
lighten the arduous labors of the Interstate Commission.
Such Governmental scrutiny would be an assurance of
justice to the railroads and safety to the people, and would,
under the lash of public opinion, soon force fractions and
unscrupulous roads into a reasonable attitude; for it would
surely develop that the road declining to co-operate in
the maintenance of proper competitive conditions "con-
templates some wrong against a competitor or the public."

CONCLUSION.

The railroads have, from the beginning and everywhere, been the great creators and distributors of the nation's wealth. They are the potent agencies which have transformed worthless and uninhabitable places into empires of wealth and population. They have wrested an empire from the wilderness and supplanted the Indian's wigwam with the white man's home more effectually than could the pioneer's rifle or the national arms. With their facilities for transportation, they have made possible and profitable the settlement of all sections of the republic, which otherwise must have been confined to a limited area along the great waterways. Their operation has made us exceptionally rich in all that goes to make a nation great and prosperous, and they are in this respect greater conquerors than the sword. *They have become the arteries of our vast commercial system, and as such are entitled to worthy recognition.* They should not have to sue as suppliants for justice ; but, their existence and encouragement ever going hand in hand with the nation's prosperity, they should be freely granted what measures of relief and protection Congress in its wisdom can yield. To the need of such measures I have aimed in this letter to call attention, so far as the limits of my subject allow.

I believe that this Government should not grant any concessions to foreign carriers that can be used to the prejudice of our domestic interests. Apropos of this point, my attention has just been called to an issue of the *Japan Daily Herald,* dated Yokohoma, 18th May, 1889, in which I find the following :

" The new Canadian Pacific line seems at last to be " getting into practical shape. On the 17th April, Mr. " Foster was to introduce into the Canadian House of " Commons, at Ottawa, three resolutions. The first " provided for a subsidy for a fortnightly line of steamers

" between British Columbia and Australia ; the second was
" to grant a subsiby of $500,000 per annum for a weekly
" fast line of steamers between Canada and the United
" Kingdom ; a contract for these has, it is since reported,
" been made with Anderson & Co., of the Orient line,
" who are to provide steamers of over twenty knots speed,
" thus bringing the termini within six days of each other.
" The third resolution provided that if Great Britain gives
" not less than £45,000 per annum for a monthly service,
" nor less than £75,000 per annum for a fortnightly
" service between British Columbia, China and Japan, the
" Governor-General in Council may, on behalf of Canada,
" add £15,000 in the one case, or £25,000 in the other,
" to the sums granted by Great Britain."

I believe that a railroad system built by a foreign power
as a military measure, and with the avowed object of
promoting trade between the provinces of the country that
created it, by withdrawing their trade from the United
States ; whose further object is, by subsidies on land and
sea, to divert from us to the Canadian route the traffic between the North American Continent and the Orient on the
one hand, and Europe on the other, as well as that between
Trans-Pacific and Trans-Atlantic countries, *should not be
favored where favors can be withheld.* It should not, for
example, be permitted to promote its cherished objects by
the use, or rather the abuse, of our custom laws regarding
transportation. These laws were intended to facilitate the
handling of exports and imports by American merchants
and carriers, and should not now be deflected to the
unpatriotic purpose of turning into Canadian channels the
current of traffic in American bonded merchandise.

I would emphasize my belief also that American carriers
should be relieved of the onerous restrictions laid upon
them by the fourth and fifth sections of the Interstate Commerce Law, so that they may not be denied any reasonable

facility to enable them to contest their own ground against invading carriers.

Finally, I think it of the utmost importance to the welfare of our people and the integrity of our institutions that this Government strenuously assert as its doctrine and policy, " Protection, not only to American industry and manufactures, but to American enterprise of whatsoever kind or nature."

Respectfully submitted,

A. N. TOWNE.

San Francisco, June 20, 1889.

www.ingramcontent.com/pod-product-compliance
Lightning Source LLC
Chambersburg PA
CBHW021635270326
41931CB00008B/1038